D1410934

CREATIVE EDUCATION

MINNESOTA VIKINGS

NFL TODAY

JULIE NELSON

Published by Creative Education
123 South Broad Street, Mankato, Minnesota 56001
Creative Education is an imprint of The Creative Company

Designed by Rita Marshall

Photos by: Allsport USA, Bettmann/CORBIS, SportsChrome

Library of Congress Cataloging-in-Publication Data

Nelson, Julie
Minnesota Vikings / by Julie Nelson.
p. cm. — (NFL today)
Summary: Traces the history of the team from its beginnings through 1999.
ISBN 1-58341-049-X

1. Minnesota Vikings (Football team)—History—Juvenile literature. [1.
Minnesota Vikings (Football team)—History. 2. Football—History.] I. Title. II.
Series: NFL today (Mankato, Minn.)

GV956.M5N45   2000
796.332'64'09776579—dc21   99-015753

First edition

9 8 7 6 5 4 3 2 1

Every winter, snow and cold descend on Minnesota like a blanket, covering the northern state until the warm sun of spring finally thaws the frozen land. It takes a special kind of person to brave the cold, but the hardy folks in Minnesota don't hibernate through the long winters. They ski, skate, ice-fish, ride snowmobiles, and gather inside the Hubert H. Humphrey Metrodome in Minneapolis to cheer on their gridiron heroes, the Minnesota Vikings.

Since entering the National Football League in 1961, the Vikings have repaid fans for their loyalty with one NFL championship, four Super Bowl appearances, and playoff

One of the first Vikings stars, running back Tommy Mason.

Rookie quarterback Fran Tarkenton tossed 18 touch-down passes.

berths in more than half of their seasons. Four former Vikings have been inducted into the Pro Football Hall of Fame, and several others are awaiting their turn. From Fran Tarkenton and Alan Page to Cris Carter and John Randle, the list of Vikings greats is a long one.

The Vikings, however, refuse to dwell on the past. In recent years, the team has retained its usual spot at or near the top of the NFC Central Division—the league's "Black-and-Blue" division—keeping Minnesota fans confident that a Super Bowl title will soon heat up the cold North.

IT ALL STARTED WITH WINTER

It is fitting that the founder of the Minnesota Vikings was a man named Winter—Max Winter. After emigrating to the United States from Austria, Winter quickly fell in love with American sports. As his business enterprises in Minnesota prospered, he used his earnings to establish a professional basketball team in Minneapolis called the Lakers, which later moved to Los Angeles.

It wasn't until 1955 that Winter saw his first pro football game. He was captivated by the energy and excitement of the game and began writing letters to the NFL commissioner seeking to establish a franchise in Minnesota. Those letters went unanswered for several years. Then, in 1959, Winter looked elsewhere and considered purchasing a franchise in the newly-founded American Football League. The risk of losing out on Minnesota brought the NFL around quickly, and in January 1960, the league awarded Winter a team.

Electrifying receiver Randy Moss.

Cornerback Ed Sharockman picked off six passes to lead the Vikings secondary.

Winter's first step in building his team was to hire a head coach. Winter first offered the job to Bud Grant, a former player on his Lakers basketball team who was also an experienced football man. When Grant turned him down, Winter hired Norm Van Brocklin, a former star NFL quarterback.

The team that Van Brocklin put on the field for Minnesota's first season in 1961 was a strange mixture of the old and the new. Among the aging veterans was Hugh McElhenny, a future Hall of Fame halfback on the downside of his career. The rookies included running back Tommy Mason, quarterback Fran Tarkenton, and cornerback Ed Sharockman. End Jim Marshall had also been acquired in a trade with Cleveland to anchor the defensive line. The Vikings had a little talent, but not much.

Despite their shallow roster, the Vikings got off to a remarkable start. In their first regular-season game, the Vikings crushed the favored Chicago Bears 37–13. That game established Fran Tarkenton as Minnesota's leader—a position he would hold for the next six years. Tarkenton entered the game in the second quarter and proceeded to throw four touchdown passes and run for a fifth score in the big win. Unfortunately, the club lost its next seven contests and finished its inaugural season with a 3–11 record.

Minnesota continued to suffer growing pains over the next few seasons. Tarkenton, meanwhile, established himself as a crowd favorite with his unique ability to scramble away from defenders until his receivers could get open.

The Vikings were far from a one-man show, however. Running back Bill Brown came to Minnesota in 1962 in a trade with the Bears and was the team's leading rusher and one of its top receivers for the next 13 years. Another offensive star was Paul Flatley, whose 51 receptions for 867 yards placed him among the league's top receivers in 1963.

When the offense stalled, Minnesota often relied on Fred Cox to produce miracles with his accurate kicks. Cox kicked for the Vikings for 15 seasons (1963–1977), and the 1,365 points he totaled still rank him among the top scorers in NFL history.

On defense, the Vikings were anchored by Jim Marshall, who occupied one end of Minnesota's defensive line for a remarkable 19 seasons. The 6-foot-4 and 240-pound wonder seemed immune to injury or illness, playing in an NFL-record 282 consecutive games.

Marshall's career had many highlights, but Vikings fans will always remember a "lowlight" that took place early in his career. In an October 1964 game against the San Francisco 49ers, Marshall scooped up a fumble and raced into the end zone before flinging the ball into the stands. Unfortunately, he had run the wrong direction; instead of scoring a touchdown for the Vikings, he had given San Francisco two points for a safety.

Luckily, Minnesota won the game anyway. The victory was one of eight the team earned during the 1964 season on its way to an 8–5–1 record, the first winning campaign in its history. That season marked the high point in Coach Van Brocklin's years in Minnesota, but during the next two years, Van Brocklin and Tarkenton continually clashed. The dissension was evident on the field, as the club fell to 4–9–1 in 1966. Soon after, Van Brocklin resigned, and Tarkenton was traded to the New York Giants.

Fred Cox kicked off his illustrious career with the Vikings, leading the team in scoring.

Two former defensive stars: tackle Keith Millard . . .

. . . and end Chris Doleman.

1 9 6 6

Halfback Dave Osborn helped the Vikings upset NFL champion Green Bay 20–17.

Choosing a replacement for Van Brocklin was an easy task for Max Winter. There was only one man he wanted to coach his team: Bud Grant. Although Grant had turned down the job in 1961, he accepted it six years later, and a long, happy relationship began.

Bud Grant came to the Vikings with an impressive resume. After playing football and basketball at the University of Minnesota, Grant joined Winter's Lakers in the National Basketball Association and then played in the NFL with the Philadelphia Eagles. He later played for, then coached, the Winnipeg Blue Bombers in the Canadian Football League (CFL), leading the team to four league championships in 10 years. His remarkable record continued after he joined Minnesota. By the time he retired in 1986, Grant had coached the Vikings for 18 seasons. His total of 168 NFL victories placed him eighth on the all-time coaching list at the time of his retirement.

Grant's Minnesota coaching career didn't start off so positively, however. The club won only three games in 1967. There were several reasons for the poor record. After Tarkenton's departure, CFL veteran quarterback Joe Kapp had been imported from Canada, but he took a while to get used to playing in the NFL. In addition, the defense had several newcomers who needed to learn the pro game, including future Hall of Fame tackle Alan Page.

The Vikings' "glory years" began the next season, when the team won its first Central Division title and qualified for the playoffs for the first time with an 8–6 record. The defensive front four of Marshall, Page, Carl Eller, and Gary Larsen—known as the "Purple People Eaters"—terrorized opposing quarterbacks and runners, while defensive backs Bobby Bryant and Paul Krause were among the league leaders in interceptions. Minnesota's first playoff run lasted only one game—a 24–14 loss to Baltimore—but the good times were just beginning.

In 1969, Joe Kapp jumpstarted the Vikings in the second game of the season by torching the Colts with an NFL-record seven touchdown passes. That began a string of 12 straight victories, leading to a second consecutive Central Division crown and another playoff berth. This time, Minnesota came back from a 10-point halftime deficit against the Los Angeles Rams to win 23–20 and reach the NFL championship game.

Stoic coach Bud Grant led the Vikings to the NFL championship.

Indestructible defensive end Jim Marshall.

Playing in eight-degree weather (a typical January day in Minnesota), the Vikings pounded the visiting Cleveland Browns 27–7 for the NFL title.

The Vikings then traveled to New Orleans to take on the Kansas City Chiefs, champions of the American Football League, in Super Bowl IV. Though they were favored by 13 points, the Vikings never got their offense in gear against the Chiefs. Minnesota's mighty defense struggled as well, and Kansas City won easily, 23–7.

Undaunted by this setback, Minnesota stayed on top of its division in both 1970 and 1971, but lost each year in the first round of the playoffs. The Purple People Eaters, meanwhile, continued to devour their opponents. In 1971, Alan Page became the first defensive lineman ever to be named the league's Most Valuable Player. But the offense needed help, particularly at quarterback.

Meanwhile, veteran quarterback Fran Tarkenton was unhappy playing in New York. Aware of the Vikings' need for a signal-caller, he asked to be traded back to Minnesota. In 1972, Tarkenton got his wish.

The Vikings were energized by Tarkenton's homecoming. In the next four years, they returned to the Super Bowl three more times and posted an incredible 45–10–1 record. Tarkenton went on to set NFL career records for pass completions (3,686), passing yardage (47,003), and touchdown passes (342). But individual honors were not that important to Tarkenton. "The records are secondary to what our team does," he once remarked. "I'm more concerned with things other than statistical charts." In 1975, Tarkenton was named the NFL's Most Valuable Player.

1 9 7 0

End Carl Eller led Minnesota in sacks (13) for the second consecutive season.

Fran Tarkenton passed his way into the Hall of Fame.

Chuck Foreman, the Vikings' all-time leading rusher.

Unfortunately, through all of the team's great years, the biggest prize of all eluded the Vikings. How could they have lost the Super Bowl all four times they made it to the big game? Vikings players and fans were haunted by that question and by those losses: 23–7 to Kansas City in 1970; 24–7 to Miami in 1974; 16–6 to Pittsburgh in 1975; and 32–14 to Oakland in 1977.

A NEW BAND OF VIKINGS

The opening of the Hubert H. Humphrey Metrodome in Minneapolis in April 1982 signaled a new era for the Vikings. The old outdoor Metropolitan Stadium in nearby Bloomington was gone, as were Tarkenton, running back Chuck Foreman, Eller, Page, and other stars of the 1970s. The team was sporting a new stadium, and it soon showed off a new generation of heroes as well.

The team's new defense featured end Doug Martin, linebackers Matt Blair and Scott Studwell, and safety Joey Browner. The offense was keyed by quarterback Tommy Kramer, running back Darrin Nelson, and tight end Steve Jordan. Despite their talent, the Vikings hovered around the .500 mark during the early 1980s, leading Bud Grant to retire after the 1983 season. In 1984, Les Steckel stepped in to replace him, and the Vikings fell to 3–13, their worst record in more than 20 years. Minnesota badly needed a change.

Unexpectedly, that change came in the form of a familiar face: Bud Grant. After agreeing to coach the Vikings for one more year, Grant turned them back in the right direction with a 7–9 record. In 1986, he turned over the reins to Jerry

1 9 8 3

Rookie safety Joey Browner made an instant mark in the NFL with his punishing tackles.

Alan Page, the leader of the feared "Purple People Eaters" (pages 18-19).

Burns, his longtime assistant, certain that the team was ready to become a winner again.

With Burns at the helm, the Vikings brought in more talent over the next several years. Key players included offensive linemen Gary Zimmerman and Randall McDaniel, quarterback Wade Wilson, defensive linemen Keith Millard and Chris Doleman, and cornerback Carl Lee. Each would earn All-Pro honors under "Burnsie's" watchful eye.

One of Minnesota's most exciting new stars was Anthony Carter. A three-time All-American at the University of Michigan, Carter quickly established himself as a superstar in Minnesota. Though small by pro football standards (5-foot-11 and 175 pounds), Carter made up for his lack of size with a "second sense" for the game. Coach Burns once remarked, "I've always said that if the good Lord put anybody on this earth to play pro football, it was AC. He just forgot to give him a body."

Carter gave the Vikings a deep threat that Minnesota quarterbacks Tommy Kramer and Wade Wilson took advantage of often. Carter's big plays helped the Vikings regain the winning touch. Minnesota went 8–7 in 1987 and made it back to the playoffs for the first time since 1982.

The Vikings continued their comeback run by crushing favored New Orleans 44–10 in the Wild Card game, with Carter scoring twice on long passes. In the second round, Minnesota dispatched the San Francisco 49ers 36–24 behind five Chuck Nelson field goals. All the Vikings needed was one more win to return to the Super Bowl for a fifth time.

The NFC championship game on January 17, 1988, proved to be a memorable battle between the Vikings and the Washington Redskins. In the fourth quarter, Washington went ahead 17–10. Wade Wilson then led the Vikings to the Washington six-yard line with less than a minute left in the game. On fourth down, however, halfback Darrin Nelson dropped a bullet pass at the goal line, and the Vikings' season came to an end.

Undaunted, Minnesota was back in the playoffs again the next two seasons. Wilson led the NFL in passing in 1988, and Carter was second in the league with 72 catches for 1,225 yards. But the club's real heroes were the defensive players such as Chris Doleman, Keith Millard, and Joey Browner, who didn't give up a single touchdown during one four-game streak. The Vikings defense continued to dominate the next season, leading the league with 71 quarterback sacks (one short of the NFL record).

Although the Vikings lost to the San Francisco 49ers in the playoffs both years, Minnesota fans figured that a new stretch of "glory years" was coming in the 1990s.

1 9 8 8

Defensive tackle Keith Millard led a fierce pass rush with eight sacks.

SAILING FOR THE TOP

Minnesota started the new decade poorly, posting a 6–10 record in 1990. But the season did have one bright note. The Vikings acquired sure-handed wide receiver Cris Carter, who had been released by the Philadelphia Eagles.

An improved 8–8 record in 1991 was not enough to earn Jerry Burns a contract renewal. Instead, the Vikings hired Stanford head coach Dennis Green to take over the team in 1992. Green, a former offensive assistant with the San Francisco 49ers, focused first on the sluggish Vikings offense.

Receiver Anthony Carter had a knack for making big plays.

With Green's guidance, the Vikings stormed back to the top of the NFC Central Division with an 11–5 record.

In 1993, Cris Carter led the offense with 86 catches for more than 1,000 yards as the Vikings earned another playoff berth. It would be the first of six straight 1,000-yard seasons for Carter. A year later, he established himself as one of the game's premier receivers by setting a new NFL record with 122 pass receptions.

Stardom didn't come easily for Cris Carter, however. Early in his pro career with the Eagles, he began abusing drugs and alcohol. Philadelphia released him in 1990, and the Vikings claimed him for $100 on waivers. In Minnesota, Carter decided to change his life. He freed himself from drugs and alcohol and became deeply religious.

Once he improved his personal life, Carter's physical talents began to shine forth as well. The 6-foot-3 receiver specialized in basketball-type "alley-oop" passes. "I always tell the quarterback, when in doubt, just throw it high and I'll go up and get it," he said.

The new quarterback taking that advice was veteran Warren Moon, who came to Minnesota in 1994 after 10 spectacular seasons in Houston. Moon put the ball in the air more than 600 times for Minnesota in 1994, completing 371 passes for 4,264 yards—new club records.

Moon was supported by a strong cast of many young standouts. Halfbacks Amp Lee and Robert Smith provided Minnesota with a solid ground attack, while Carter and Jake Reed were among the best receiving duos in the league. The Vikings defense—led by relentless All-Pro tackle John Randle—was strong as well.

In his first season with the Vikings, Warren Moon led Minnesota to the division crown.

Tackle John Randle terrorized quarterbacks, finishing the year with a team-high 10.5 sacks.

Neither the Vikings offense nor the defense was clicking early in 1995, however, and the club started slowly. A loss to Cincinnati in the season finale dropped Minnesota to an 8–8 record and cost the Vikings another trip to the playoffs.

Led by the strong debut season of quarterback Brad Johnson, the Vikings improved to 9–7 in 1996. Although the Vikings stumbled in the postseason, getting drubbed 40–15 by the defending Super Bowl champion Dallas Cowboys in the first round, Minnesota had found its new starting quarterback. Moon moved on to Seattle, and another veteran quarterback—Randall Cunningham—filled the backup role.

For 11 seasons, Cunningham had played in Philadelphia, earning a reputation as one of the fastest, most athletic quarterbacks in NFL history. Although he had retired after the

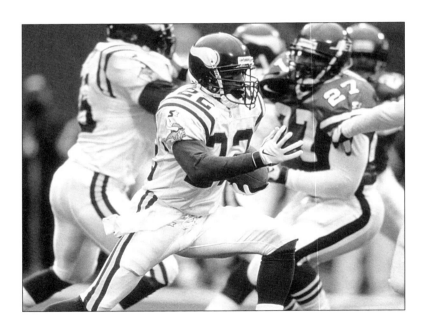

Speedy punt return star David Palmer.

1995 season, the Vikings thought his skills were still intact and brought him on board. When Johnson suffered a neck injury late in the 1997 season, Cunningham's second career in the NFL took off. He started the final three regular-season games for the Vikings before leading them to one of the most thrilling comebacks in franchise history.

At halftime of Minnesota's Wild Card playoff matchup against the New York Giants, the Vikings trailed 19–3. With less than two minutes to go, however, Cunningham connected with receiver Jake Reed to make the score 22–20. After Minnesota recovered an onside kick, Cunningham marched the Vikings down the field before Eddie Murray drilled the game-winning field goal with only 10 seconds left. Stunned Giants fans looked on as Minnesota celebrated its first playoff victory since 1988.

Although the Vikings were overpowered a week later by San Francisco, the victory in New York seemed to be a positive omen. No one knew it yet, but Minnesota was about to embark on a season for the record books.

1 9 9 7

Linebacker Ed McDaniel led the defense with 135 total tackles.

PURPLE PRIDE

In 1998, "Purple Pride" was reborn in Minnesota thanks in large part to two new arrivals. One was a 70-year-old car salesman from Texas, and the other was a lanky 21-year-old wide receiver.

Billionaire Red McCombs, who started making his fortune with a single car dealership in 1957, bought the Vikings franchise in July 1998. With his contagious enthusiasm and prediction of a perfect 16–0 season, McCombs raised football

Receiver Cris Carter, a future Hall-of-Famer (pages 26-27).

25

Gary Anderson made 94 kicks in a row during the regular season.

excitement in Minnesota to a fever pitch. Fortunately, the Vikings had just acquired a young star who would match that level of excitement on the field: Randy Moss.

Although he had racked up impressive statistics in two seasons at Marshall University and been a Heisman Trophy candidate, Moss was considered a risky gamble as the 1998 NFL draft approached. As a teenager, he had run into frequent problems with the law. Although the 6-foot-4 receiver ran the 40-yard dash in less than 4.3 seconds, 19 NFL teams passed on Moss before the Vikings drafted him. Moss vowed to make those teams pay. When asked what he wanted to achieve as a rookie, he replied, "whatever I can to rip this league up."

Moss did just that in 1998. He shattered NFL rookie records with 17 touchdowns and 1,313 receiving yards, earning All-Pro honors. Moss's combination of speed, size, leaping ability, and natural instincts made him the most feared game-breaker in the league. Cris Carter, Moss's mentor both on and off the field, explained, "You know that deer-in-the-headlights look that rookies get? Randy doesn't get that."

With Moss added to an already potent lineup that included Cunningham, Carter, Jake Reed, Robert Smith, and a huge offensive line, the Vikings offense became virtually unstoppable. Over the course of the season, Minnesota scored a total of 556 points, shattering the old NFL record for most points in a season. The Vikings cruised to a 15–1 record, then dispatched Arizona 41–21 in the playoffs to move on to the NFC championship game.

Playing in front of a deafening home crowd in the Metrodome, the Vikings roared out to a 20–7 lead over the underdog Atlanta Falcons. Several Minnesota turnovers and a resilient Atlanta defense, however, kept the Falcons close.

With only minutes remaining in the game and Minnesota up 27–20, the Vikings drove to the Atlanta 20-yard line. They then called on Gary Anderson—who had not missed a single kick all season—to kick the game-clinching field goal. As 64,000 Minnesota fans confidently looked on, Anderson missed. The Falcons then quickly scored to tie the game at 27–27 and force sudden-death overtime. Minnesota's offense, seemingly stunned by the turn of events, stalled on two drives in overtime before Falcons kicker Morten Andersen booted the game-winning field goal.

The Vikings and their fans were devastated—what had seemed like destiny had turned into disaster. "I don't really care too much about what happened this season—the records and all," Moss said dejectedly after the bitter loss. "The Super Bowl is something you dream of as a kid, and we had an opportunity to get there. . . . We let it slip right out of our hands."

The stinging loss seemed to affect Minnesota early in the 1999 season, as the Vikings started a mere 2–4. Once journeyman quarterback Jeff George stepped in to replace a struggling Cunningham, however, the Vikings offense took off. Robert Smith topped 1,000 rushing yards again, Cris Carter enjoyed one of the finest seasons of his career, and Randy Moss continued to tear through defenses despite almost constant double-team coverage. Minnesota stormed to wins in eight of its last 10 games to stake a playoff claim.

After destroying the Dallas Cowboys 27–10 in the first round of the playoffs, the Vikings marched into St. Louis to

1 9 9 9

Guard Randall McDaniel made his team-record 11th straight Pro Bowl appearance.

Aggressive linebacker Dwayne Rudd.

A punishing hitter, safety Robert Griffith.   31

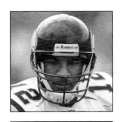

2 0 0 1

Vikings fans looked for quarterback Daunte Culpepper to lead the team's aerial attack.

take on the surprising new NFC powerhouse, the St. Louis Rams, in a clash of powerful offenses. Although Minnesota led 17–14 at halftime, the Rams turned several second-half Vikings turnovers into a scoring explosion, pulling away to win in a 49–37 shootout.

The Vikings' turbulent season continued even after the playoffs, as many members of the team's coaching staff quit or were fired. Salary limitations also forced the team to release several star players, including future Hall of Fame guard Randall McDaniel. "Randall McDaniel's the only football player to ever have a 190–0 record," said Vikings longsnapper Mike Morris. "There's never been a game when, after four quarters are over, an opposing player could say to himself, 'I beat Randall McDaniel today.'"

Despite the changes, the Vikings should continue to reign near the top of the NFC for years to come. With Coach Green leading one of the NFL's best offenses, this historic franchise may soon earn the Super Bowl championship that has eluded it for so long.

32